Max Miller was not only a legend in his own lifetime, he has remained one ever since. His outrageous stage costume (multi-coloured plus-fours, a white trilby hat and two-tone shoes) was matched by his startlingly racy patter and his cheerfully risqué songs. He was at the top for most of his life – the uncrowned Emperor of the many Empires he filled to capacity whenever he appeared on the bill.

His jokes have gone into the folklore of bawdy British humour and his admiring imitators can still stop the show with fortissimo Millerisms.

The best of Max Miller's jokes, asides, songs and anecdotes have been assembled for the first time in this collection aptly titled *The Max Miller Blue Book*. Lionel Hale described him as the 'pure gold of the Music Hall', and as Max himself said – 'Miller's the name, lady. There'll never be another.'

**Barry Took** was for some years a Music Hall comedian and revue artist, though he is perhaps better known as a writer of comedy scripts for radio and television ('Round the Horne', 'Marty', 'The World of Beachcomber', 'Rowan and Martin's Laugh In', among others). A frequent broadcaster and occasional journalist, he has recently become the scriptwriter of the long-running Flook comic strip in the *Daily Mail*.

**Trog** (Wally Fawkes) is the *Observer*'s political cartoonist and creator of Flook in the *Daily Mail*.

# The
# Max Miller
# Blue Book

# THE MAX MILLER BLUE BOOK

Compiled by Barry Took

Illustrations by Trog

 Robson Books

First published in Great Britain in 1975 by Robson
Books Ltd., 28 Poland Street, London W1V 3DB.
Copyright (c) 1975 Robson Books and Barry Took.
ISBN 0 903895 53 6.

The publishers would like to thank Mrs Kathleen
Miller for her kind cooperation in the preparation of
this book. Acknowledgments are also due to the following: The Peter Maurice Music Co. Ltd for 'Mary from
the Dairy' (copyright © 1950, words and music by
Max Miller/Sam Kern/James Walsh); Mr Billy Merrin
for 'Be Sincere'; Mrs Gladys G. Keeping for 'She Shall
Have Music Wherever She Goes'; Ellis Ashton (British
Music Hall Society) for the theatre poster and photo on
p.11; Fox Photos Ltd. for the photo on p.8.

Designed by Timothy Jaques FSIA

Printed in Great Britain by Hazell Watson & Viney Ltd, Aylesbury, Bucks

# FINSBURY PARK

## MOSS' Empire THEATRE

Proprietors MOSS' EMPIRES Ltd.
Chairman PRINCE LITTLER    Managing Director VAL PARNELL    Telephone CANONBURY 2248   Manager DAVID W. WILMOT

**MONDAY, MARCH 22**

**6.25** TWICE NIGHTLY **8.40**

# MAX

### THE ONE AND ONLY

# MILLER

The New Decca Vocal Recording Star

# JOAN REGAN

New Crazy Funster

**KAY KORTZ & EUGENE**

**BILL MAYNARD**

# SCOTT SANDERS

In Old Philosophie

**BILL WAREHAM**
& BARBARA In the Balance

Dance Time with

**DENIS BROTHERS & JUNE**

In Selections from Her Top Sellers
RICOCHET
RAGGABONE MAN
TILL THEY'VE ALL GONE HOME

Danish Brother & Sister

**LIZZET & EDDIE**

Danish Brother & Sister

AERIAL THRILLS

# THE MONTONS

# Introduction

It's not easy to define precisely what it was that made Max Miller the folk hero he became in his lifetime or the legend he's become since. He certainly told rude jokes, but no ruder than those of many other comedians. He dressed in garish splendour, but so have others. He was cheeky but no cheekier than, say, Tommy Trinder or Jimmy Wheeler.

On stage, Max Miller created an atmosphere of cocky, good-natured arrogance which, harnessed to sexual themes, as his jokes almost always were, seemed to defy respectability in the way that free fall parachutists seem to defy the laws of gravity. Like the sky diver who delays pulling the rip cord till the last second, so Miller would tantalize his audience with the possibility of his saying the unsayable until at last he'd swerve past the tag of his joke with a cry of "Ere, listen!' and then, like Muhammed Ali after a victory in the ring telling his audience how great he is, he'd shout at his rapt listeners, 'Miller's the name! There'll never be another will there? They don't make 'em today.' And indeed they don't. It's strange that even now, over twelve years after his death, there are more myths about Max Miller than there are facts.

Every really dirty joke has at one time or another been attributed to him and there was a period when every saloon bar funny man would preface a story with – 'Here, this is the one Max Miller got fined for' or 'This one got Max Miller banned by the BBC'. The banned joke went something like: 'I was up this mountain and I was edging along this narrow ledge – it was so narrow there was only room for one – side-saddle – so anyway, suddenly I saw this beautiful girl coming towards me – along this ledge. There was no room to pass. Honestly, I didn't know whether to block her passage or toss myself off.'

The point is not really whether Miller ever actually told the story but that people believed he did and that they thus felt licensed to tell it themselves. It cropped up again recently when the *Guardian* television critic, Nancy Banks Smith, quoted a slightly garbled version in her column.

When Miller used to say of himself 'there'll never be another', it was the simple truth. He was unique.

My first memory of seeing the man Lionel Hale described as 'the pure gold of the Music Hall' was at Finsbury Park Empire in 1939. I was eleven years old at the time and any visit to the theatre was an adventure. At that age I didn't really understand what he was saying, of course, or rather the implications of his patter were beyond me, but I do remember vividly the electrifying effect Miller had on the audience. The band struck up his signature tune, 'Mary from the

Dairy', and Miller strutted on to a deafening shout of delight from the audience. They had something to shout at. He wore an extraordinary long fur coat over gaudy plus-fours, and a white trilby hat, and he carried a 'diamond'-topped walking stick. He strutted to the centre of the stage and stood there laughing at the audience until their clamour subsided, then, rotating his stick so that the light twinkled on the simulated diamond, he said, 'Look, that's nice isn't it lady? I'm filthy with money –' he paused and added, 'I'm filthy without it.' That brought the place down. The audience knew that their hero had come home. More was to follow. He took his overcoat off and hung it on an invisible hook on the backcloth and revealed the most startling garment in the history of sartorial anarchy. It was a suit of plus-fours and to say it was a riot of colour would be a limp understatement. It was a rainbow creation made of silky material which shimmered in the spotlight. He pirouetted to show it to its maximum advantage – more laughter – and then, to a lady in the front stalls already convulsed, he said, 'D'you like it, gel? Nice, isn't it? No, it is. It's nice. Would you like a feel?' His whole approach was a mixture of impudence and indignation. 'It's people like you that give me a bad name!' he'd shout when some audacious piece of *double entendre* had hit the mark. 'Filthy lot! Filthy lot!' he'd cry when they got the point of a story before he'd quite completed it. 'I'll tell you this one, then we'll all get nicked,' he'd confide.

'There'll never be another' just about says it. There won't. I guess there *can't* be another Max Miller. But how much of this was the stage persona and how much the man himself? I worked with Max Miller only once on a radio Music Hall programme and we shared a dressing-room at the BBC's Playhouse Studio. He, of course, was the top of the bill and I was one of the supporting acts. I found him quiet, polite, reserved and charming. We chatted the generalities of show business, wished each other well for the broadcast, and afterwards a short flurry of mutual congratulation terminated with the now soberly-clad Miller hurrying off to catch the train to his home in Brighton. It seemed to me then, as it does now, that he kept his mischief and his extraordinary technicolour personality strictly for the performance.

While in the outside world the myths of his daring and racy indifference to the law abounded, in show business his reputation was that of a tough businessman who was, not to put too fine a point on it, mean. I've known stage managers of Variety theatres gloomily prophesy that the traditional tip would be small or non-existent when Miller topped the bill, but at Wood Green Empire in 1949 he literally showered silver on the stage crew at the end of the week. I worked the lighting switchboard there that year and saw most of the then top comedians in action, and good though Arthur Askey, Vic Oliver, Harry Mooney and the others were, no one quite had the onstage charisma that Miller generated.

Max Miller was born Thomas Henry Sargent in Brighton in 1895. He ran away from home to join the original Billy Smart's Circus, and became a solo entertainer whilst in the army in the First World War. In the post-war years he quickly evolved as the 'Cheeky Chappie' and became in due course the highest-paid Variety entertainer of his day, a frequent broadcaster, a Royal Command performer and a film star. He was almost a permanent fixture at the Holborn Empire until it was bombed in 1940, and appeared almost as frequently at the London Palladium. When, after the Second World War, the London Casino became for a time a Variety theatre, he topped the bill there too, regaling the audience with the saga of the sisters Annie and Fanny. 'Annie's the one with her teeth in, Fanny's the one with them out', and confiding that he'd like to marry them both – and 'When I've tied the knot with what little I've got I'll see that they both get a share.'

The London Casino had no Music Hall tradition as the older Empires did and the audiences were more 'West End', but as people who remember Max Miller there at the time say, 'No matter how refined or pompous the audience were, within two or three minutes he'd have them laughing their heads off and leaning forward in their seats so as not to miss a word or a nuance of his incredible patter.'

Not that Miller was noted for nuance as, for instance, when he peeled a banana counting the skins as he did so – 'One skin, two skin, three skin . . . here, lady – want a bite ?'

Whatever Miller was as a comedian, he certainly wasn't furtive.

The innuendo in most of his jokes was as plain as the nose on your face and his great skill was to allow his audience to make the connection themselves.

> *'I like the girls who do,*
> *I like the girls who don't;*
> *I hate the girl who says she will*
> *And then she says she won't.*
> *But the girl that I like best of all*
> *And I think you'll say I'm right –*
> *Is the one who says she never has*
> *But looks as though she . . . .*
>     *'Ere, listen . . . '*

Max's great invention was the Blue Book. He'd pull two books from his pocket, one white, the other blue. Then he'd tell the audience, 'In the White Book they're all clean jokes and in the Blue Book there's all the others. Which do you want – the White Book or the Blue Book?' The audience would shout their unanimous choice – 'The Blue Book, Max – the *Blue* Book.'

In today's debased coinage Miller would be called a super-star – he was certainly a superlative performer. His timing was as sharp as a razor, his grasp of what his audience wanted absolute and his ability to give them just that uncanny.

I think that what made Max Miller a legend was his ability to make sex a cheerful business, something to enjoy, be happy about, and above all something that *gave* pleasure.

That's why he was loved and that's why he's remembered – he said the things we wanted to hear and when he said them, somehow, magically, they became true. As he used to sing:

> *'Laugh and be happy,*
> *I'm your Cheeky Chappie –*
> *It's funny what a smile can do.'*

BARRY TOOK
25 June 1975

*Compiler's Note*
The material in *The Max Miller Blue Book* has been compiled from various sources. It is what Max Miller said and sang over a period from 1939 to 1959, and while it represents only a part of his prodigious repertoire, it is completely authentic. It is what he said, as he said it, and has been edited only in the interests of clarification.

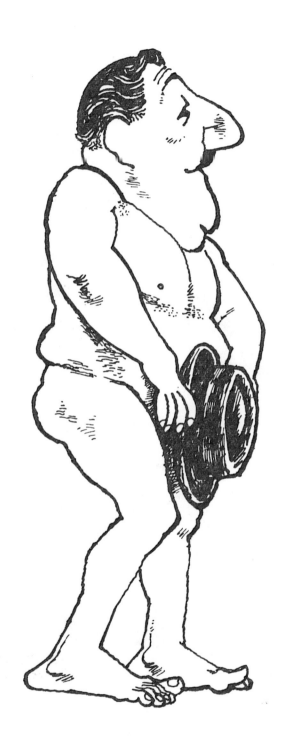

'ere!

# Mary from the Dairy

*I fell in love with Mary from the Dairy,*
*But Mary wouldn't fall in love with me;*
*Down by an old mill stream*
*We both sat down to dream:*

*That was when I offered her my strawberries and cream,*
*We walked and talked together in the moonlight,*
*She asked me what I knew of farmery,*
*I said, 'Mary, I'm no fool,*
*You can't milk Barney's Bull,*
*That's when Mary from the dairy fell for me.*

*Little did she know that I was thinking up a scheme,*
*The wife she says that she is going to leave me,*
*The moment that she does then I am free,*
*There's a little girl I know*
*I'll take her and I'll show,*
*Where Mary from the Dairy fell for me.*

VARIATION

*'Now on our farm,' said Mary from the dairy,*
*'We've got the finest cows you've ever seen.*
*I don't do things by halves –*
*I'll let you see my calves,*
*And they're not the same shape calves as Nellie Dean's.'*

Now, I've got two books, I've got a White Book and a Blue Book – and by that you can gather that I've got two sorts of stories. I'm going to tell you one out of the White Book first:

**'Why did the chicken cross the road? – For some fowl reason!'**

Here's another one from the White Book:

**'There was a little girl**
**Who had a little curl**
**Right in the middle of her forehead,**
**And when she was good she was very very good**
**And when she was bad she was very very popular.'**

It says in the White Book – 'A mother of eight – a mother of eight – sat up late stitching her husband's pyjamas. See page 4, Blue Book.'

Here's the answer: 'A stitch in time saves nine.'

I'd better stay on the Blue Book:

**'Adam and Eve in the Garden dwelt,**
**They were so happy and jolly;**
**I wonder how they would have felt**
**If all the leaves had been holly.'**

And that reminds me, Eve was a wonderful woman. All she wore was a fig leaf. Can you imagine a woman walking down the main street with just a fig leaf on ? She'd probably get a touch of prickly heat!

Now, there was a woman, Eve – what a terrible woman – dead jealous. She was so jealous that when Adam came home at night she used to count his ribs.

Did you hear about the fellow who came home one night and his wife had got two black eyes? He said, 'Where did you get the black eyes?' She said, 'The lodger gave them to me.' He said, 'The lodger?' She said, 'Yes.' He said, 'Where's the lodger?' She said, 'Upstairs.' He shouted upstairs, he said, 'Did you give my wife two black eyes?' The lodger said, 'Yes.' He said, 'What for?' The lodger said, 'I found out she was unfaithful to us.'

Listen. A fellow took his wife to Paris – there's a novelty to start with. It's foolish – like taking coals to Newcastle. No, but I mean, they've got a lot of coal up there, haven't they? He took his wife to Paris – they were walking along the boulevard one morning when all of a sudden she saw a hat in a shop window. She said, 'John, I like the hat. Buy it for me.' He said, 'No. I don't want to spend a lot of money, I'll buy you a hat when we get back to London.' She said, 'No, buy me this one 'cos I like it. It's nice, it'll suit me.' He said, 'No, don't waste any time, ducky, let's go for a walk.' So they went for a walk and as they were walking along he saw a red lamp, see. So he turned to the wife, he said, 'You still fancy the hat?' She said, 'Yes.' He said, 'Well, here's a pound, go and get it. And take your time.' So she went to get the hat, he went towards the red lamp, and when he got there it turned green.

I met a pal of mine the other day. I said, 'Charlie, they tell me that you're married now.' He said, 'That's right.' I said, 'Well, now you know what's what.' He said, 'What?' I said, 'Now you know what's what'. He said, 'What do you mean?' I said, 'Well, if you're married you must know what's what.' He said, 'I think you're crazy.' And he started walking home, and as he was walking home he kept saying to himself, 'Now you're married, now you know what's what.' Well, when he got home that night he got into the bedroom and his wife was in bed, so he took all his clothes off, and he switched the light out. He didn't want to get out again, scc. And he was in the dark, and he was feeling around in the dark, y'see. And all of a sudden he said, 'What's that?' And the wife said, 'What's what?'

   *– And there it was on the mantelpiece all the time!*

It's all clever stuff, you know, this is . . .

Listen. A fellow was ploughing a field – got halfway through the field and he broke his plough, and he said to himself, 'It doesn't matter, I can borrow Charlie Smith's. He only lives about five miles away and I can walk it in two or three weeks.' So he started to walk and as he was walking along, after he'd been about three miles, he said to himself, 'I don't think he'll lend it to me. No, I feel sure he won't lend it to me. He's that kind of a man. He wouldn't lend anything to anybody.' And he kept walking and walking and talking to himself, 'He won't lend it to me, I know he won't.' Well, when he got to the door he knocked on the door and Charlie Smith came to the door, and this fellow looked straight at him and he said, 'You know where you can stick your plough.'

I was standing at the bar the other day and there was a fellow there eating olives on a string. Eating olives on a string! I said, 'What are you eating them like that for?' He said, 'I may not like 'em.'

Now there's a soldier, a soldier standing in the dock. The judge is at the back – the jury over there, the defending counsel down here. The judge said to the soldier, 'This is a very serious case, we shall have to hold it in camera.' And the soldier said, 'What does that mean?' And the judge said, 'It won't make any difference to you. The jury, they know what it means; the defending counsel, he knows what it means; and I know what it means. Clear the court.' And he said to the soldier, 'Tell me exactly what happened.' So the soldier said, 'Well,' he said, 'I met the girl,' he said, 'and she asked me to see her home, and told me she lived out in the country. Well, I took her the short way, across the field, and when I got to the centre of the field I don't know what came over me, but I got hold of her – no rough stuff – no, no rough stuff – that came later, see. And I started to kiss her and she passed out, she passed right out, then after that it was all la-di-da-di-da.' And the judge said, 'All what?' The soldier said, 'All la-di-da-di-da.' And the judge said, 'What does that mean?' The soldier said, 'Well, the jury, *they* know what it means; and the defending counsel, *he* knows what it means; and if you'd been there with your camera, *you'd* have known.'

He's a boy, isn't he, eh? Hope so. Well, how can you tell – you can't tell – you can't *tell* – you can change over night.

(GUITAR CHORDS)

That's nice, Maxie. That *is* nice. I like that, Maxie. Oh, Maxie. (PLAYS A BUM STRING) That's down, is it, Ivor? Must be the cold weather. Well, here's the first song, a song entitled 'The Girls Who Do'. Shall I start it off, Ivor, shall I start it off? Yes, I'll start it off and you'll creep in, won't you? He'll creep in – I'll give you the key.

No, well, he might be home before me, see.

# The Girls Who Do

I ne-ver fall in love With the first girl that I meet, I

like to find out first If she lives down my street. I

play the wait-ing game, On that you may de—pend, To

find the girl I'm look-ing for, I'll get her in the end. I

don't like a girl too short, I don't like a girl too tall, As

long as she's a sport, For me she's bound to fall. I

don't like a girl with brains, I much pre-fer a dunce Who'll

stop me and buy one—She'd like to try one—And I'll try an-y-thing

once!

# Here!

## More? More?

## Worse? Worse?

I don't care – I don't care –

No, well, I don't.

I don't like the girls who paint
Their cheeks just like a rose,
They may look what they ain't
With powder on their nose.

They're painting their toenails –
The thing that makes me vex'
Is the way they're dressing,
They've got me guessing –
I wonder what they're going to paint nex'!

– Here! More ? Here's one, here's one – listen:

I don't like a girl a bit
Stuck up and brags a lot,
And says that she's got it
What the others haven't got.

They all look alike to me,
I'm meeting her tonight,
If she's got that what she thinks is it
Then I think I'll be all right!

# The Hiking Song

A boy took his girl to the sea-side ——
One Sun-day morn in Ju — ly; —— They
had-n't seen much of each oth-er, —— So
sun bath-ing they thought they'd try. —— With
on — ly sea —weed for a cos-tume, —— They
lay on the sands all the day; —— But
now they've seen more of each oth-er —— 'Cos the
tide washed the sea-weed a — way. ——

A boy and a girl went out hiking,
Of course, they were both wearing shorts;
They stopped at the old Pig and Whistle,
And there had a couple of ports.

When they got back the same evening,
The neighbours all started to quiz,
For he came home late wearing her shorts –
She came home late wearing his.

Down on the farm in the country
A funny thing happened one day,
The hen and the rooster were talking,
Here's what they both had to say:

Said the rooster, 'I can't understand it,
You used to lay eggs by the score.'
Said the hen, 'Well, old cock, I can't help it –
You don't come around any more.'

One day a girl she was bathing,
The maid said, 'Here comes Mr Tree';
She said, 'All right, bring him here to me –
He's quite safe, the poor chap can't see.'

She stood there like beautiful Venus,
When into the bathroom walked Jack.
He said, 'I have just come to tell you –
Today I got my eyesight back.'

An old man of ninety got married,
The bride was so young and so bold,
In his car they both went honeymooning –
She married the old man for gold.

A year later he was a daddy,
At ninety he still had the knack;
He took one look at the baby –
And then gave the chauffeur the sack.

I used to be a swimming instructor myself, at Brighton. I used to take the girls out and teach them to swim, if they couldn't swim. If they could swim, I wouldn't go out with them, I've got no time to waste. And I remember many years ago in the middle of July, I took a young lady out. She couldn't swim – I went out three miles with her – I don't mess about on the shore. When I got right out, I said to this beautiful woman, I said, 'Now what would you like to do?' She said, 'I'd like to do the breast stroke to start with.' I said, 'Well, go on, I'll stand and watch you.' So I stood on me stilts and she did the breast stroke, then she said, 'Now I think I'll turn over.' And as she turned over – may the sand get in my eyes if I tell a lie – as she turned over I slipped my hand underneath to hold her up, otherwise she'd go down – and I'm entitled to do that 'cos I'm a swimming instructor, y'see. I've got my hand underneath – she's lying on her back on the top of the water – head would be about there – her feet there – my hand would be about – about – Now, shut up – no, well . . . I've lost me place now, listen, listen, listen. And all of a sudden she gave a scream – not a very loud scream – she went, 'Ooh, ooh' – twice. But I didn't hear her the first time, I was creeping up on her. I said, 'What are you screaming for?' She said, 'A shrimp's bitten me.' I said, 'Don't be a mug, it's me,' I said, 'You want confidence.' She said, 'You want handcuffs!' – Now listen!

So I left her. When I got on the shore she started to wave to me. So I went out again. I said, 'What's the matter?' She said, 'You know that two-piece suit I was wearing?' I said, 'Yes.' She said, 'I've lost the top half. What shall I do?' I said, 'Keep going in and out with the tide.'

The following day, I took her sister out. It's according to their age how far I go out. She was thirty-five, her sister; I went out seven miles with her. And when I got out seven miles I looked at this beautiful woman – thirty-five – just going grey – on the turn, she was. She started to cry. I said, 'What are you crying for? Have you done any-thing wrong?' She said, 'No.' I said, 'Why haven't you?' Thirty-five. She said, 'I've got the cramp.' It's a shocking thing to get the cramp seven miles out in the water. It's all right in the bedroom – you can get up and walk round, can't you? Just shift the bed from

the door. She said, 'Tow me back.' So I got a ship and towed her back and I got on the shore and when I got on the shore I put her in a tent. And just as I was leaving the tent she put her hand out of the tent. She said, 'You'd better come in and massage my leg.' I said, 'If I go in there and massage your leg I shall get the sack.'

. . . I got the sack all right . . .

*no, listen...*
*Filthy lot!*

*Filthy!*

Are you enjoying the Blue Book? Are you? *This* is the book – *this* is where we all get pinched. I don't care, I'll go. I've been before – I have. I won't walk – I'll make 'em get the barrow out! I'm still on the Blue Book – listen:

**'Jack and Jill went up the hill**
**On a Sunday morning,**
**Jill came running down again,**
**She heard the gypsy's warning.'**

or . . .

'Jack and Jill went up the hill
Just like two cock linnets,
Jill came down with half a crown –
She wasn't up there two minutes.' – Here!

– and another . . .

'She was but a village maiden
Who's to say she was to blame?
But alas a wicked squire
Took away her honest name.

So she journeyed up to London
Seeking to forget her shame,
When another wicked squire
Took away her other name!'


*and* another . . .

'Mary had a little lamb
With calves as big as yours,
And everywhere that Mary went
She had to wear plus-fours.'


'Mary had a little lamb
Who acted very silly,
She plucked the wool from off its back
And smacked its piccadilly.'

Here's another . . .

**'Mary had a little bear**
**To which she was so kind**
**I've often seen her bear in front –'**

*– I'll move on to the next section –*

Listen, I was
in Spain four years ago,
and in Spain all the girls they
wear little knives in the top of their
stockings. I found that out. So
I said to myself, I'll find out exactly
what the idea is, so I said, 'What's
the idea, wearing a knife in the top
of your stocking?' She said, 'That's to
defend my honour.' I said, 'What?
A little tiny knife like that?'

I said, 'If you were in Brighton you'd want a set of carvers!'

I love animals – No, I do, honest. The other day I went to buy a racehorse. I wanted to buy a two-year-old so I went to these stables and this man said, 'I've got just the horse you're looking for.' So I went inside and there was the horse lying on the floor with a lot of blankets and sheets covering him up. He said, 'That horse'll cost you some money.' I said, 'It's dead, isn't it?' He said, 'No.' I said, 'How much do you want for it?' He said, 'A pound.' I said, 'A pound?' I said, 'Blimey, he hasn't got any shoes on.' He said, 'Well, he's not up yet.'

Well, eventually I got the horse outside and I tried to get on, and every time I tried to get on he started to kick. And he kicked so hard he got his foot in the stirrup. Got his foot in the stirrup! I said, 'Listen, if you're going to get on, I'm getting off.'

Well, I got on the horse and it fell down. So I picked it up – 'cos I'm a hefty lad, y'see. Well, I got on again and it fell down again, and I told the man – I said, 'This horse is no good to me. Every time I get on he falls down. But look, you've got some nice horses there. You've got about eight or nine in a string.' I said, 'I'll have the one in the middle.' He said, 'Don't take the one in the middle, he's propping the other ones up.'

But now a song. Mr Conductor, give me a bar and two barmaids and shuffle and cut twice, will you? (PIANO ARPEGGIO.) That's clever. Isn't that clever? The way he ran up on the piano. Right up to the top, he went. Marvellous, isn't he? Can he go down? Can he? You'll keep him on, won't you? He's clever, isn't he? Yes. Give me the opening again. Yes – a wide opening. 'Cos I'm going to sing a little number entitled 'She Shall Have Music Wherever She Goes'.

# She Shall Have Music Wherever She Goes

*Now she shall have music wherever she goes,*
*Wherever she goes,*
*Wherever she goes.*
*When she's mixing a salad*
*I'll sing her a ballad,*
*And she shall have music wherever she goes.*

*I'll play on the harp*
*When she does exercises*
*Like bending and touching her toes,*
*And when she goes upstairs*
*To do her daily dozen*
*I'll fiddle away there*
*With her pretty cousin,*
*Oh, she shall have music wherever she goes.*

Do you know what I've got in here? Do you know what I've got? It's
not me gas mask – it's not me gas mask. Hitler's secret weapon, I've got
in here. **LOOK!**

𝕬 𝕲𝖊𝖗𝖒𝖆𝖓
𝕾𝖆𝖚𝖘𝖆𝖌𝖊!

I know exactly what you're saying to yourselves – you're saying 'Why's he dressed like that?' I'll tell you why I'm dressed like this, I'm an ARP warden and when I finish here tonight I go straight on duty. I was out last night, lady, and I'm going out again tonight, ducky. No, no, I want to go out every night if I can, see. After the war as well, if I can. It's a grand alibi for we married men, innit, eh? Eight o'clock and away I go with me stirrup pump – well, I don't take any sand – no sand. Gets in between yer toes, dunnit – here, listen! I'm on duty.

– And talking about duty, that reminds me. I was on duty the other night, in the early hours of the morning. I heard footsteps and I said, 'Halt, who goes there?' And I got no reply. So I said, 'Halt, who goes there?' Still no reply. I said, 'This is your third and last chance – halt, who goes there?' And a female voice said, 'Well, you can't expect me to say "friend" after the way you treated me last night, can you?'

I bet nobody'll bump into me in a blackout. Do you like these black nights, ducky, do you like 'em, lady? No, no – they're nice, ain't they, ducky? I don't care, I don't care how dark it is – I don't care. I like it. All dark and no petrol – I don't want any petrol. I didn't ask for any. I don't. Before the war I used to take 'em out in the country – it's any doorway now!

Last night I had fun. I went out and I saw a light up in a lady's room. I shouted up, I said, 'Put that light out!' She said, 'What?' I said, 'Put that light out!' She said, 'You come and put it out, you left it on.' You've got to be careful, haven't you?

Did you see in the paper that the women are doing the men's jobs now? All the women are doing it now. Here – oh, shut up – no, well ... Well, it's not nice.


Now, in Brighton there's a woman, in Brighton there's a woman, she's cleaning windows – that's a man's job, innit, cleaning windows, innit – it's a man's job. Right on top of a ladder, five storeys high. And they say it's unlucky to walk under a ladder – here! I'd like half a chance!

The last time I was in London there was a raid – and I don't like raids, honest – no, when that warning goes my tummy goes right over, honest. No, I can't help it, I can't help it, y'see. Goes right over – and I'll run in anybody's house. Never made a bloomer yet, I'm not kidding. An' this particular night, they were dropping 'em all over the place, dropping all over the place they were. And there was a fellow running down the street in his shirt. That's all he had on – a little tiny shirt – running down the street. I said, 'Where are you going?' He said, 'I can't stand this – I'm going home.'

# – Now, Listen!

Now, I started courting when I was seventeen, honest, when I was seventeen. I was in the kitchen, I shall never forget it if I live that long; I was in the kitchen brushing my hair back, putting on a clean collar three inches high – the collar – looked like I had my ears off. And me mother said, 'Where're you going?' I said, 'I'm going courting.' She said, 'You're going what?' I said, 'I'm going courting.' She said, 'You're going to bed.' Dead wicked, dead wicked, me mother. What a crafty woman, eh? She said, 'Get up those stairs.' Honest, she sent me to bed with no supper! She said, 'You'll get no supper but a piece of bread and butter – one slice.' Later on when my father came in, he said, 'Where's Maxie?' She said, 'I caught him in the kitchen making supper, said he was going courting – I send him to bed.' He said, 'What?' She said, 'I've sent him to bed. I gave him a slice of bread and butter.' He said, 'Where's the frying pan?' She said, 'You're not going to hit him with that, are you?' He said, 'No, I'm going to fry him a piece of steak – you can't go courting on bread and butter!'

I remember the first time I went to a dance. I said to a young lady, 'Can I see you home?' She said, 'I don't allow boys to take me home.' I said, 'Why not?' She said, 'Last night I let Johnny Smith take me home. I said, 'You should be proud that he took you home because his father is a self-made man. And you can imagine the struggle he had.'

She said, 'Can you imagine the struggle *I* had?' – Here!

Now what I want to tell you is this. Before I was married I was courting my wife ten years. Before I was married. Then I went round to see her father. And I looked straight at him. He said, 'Hello.' I said, Hello.' He said, 'What do you want?' I said, 'I've been courting your daughter for ten years.' He said, 'So what?' I said, 'I want to marry her.' He said, 'I thought you wanted a pension.' He said, 'If you marry my daughter, I'll give you three acres and a cow.'

*You're quite right – you're quite right. I'm still waiting for the three acres.*

No, well perhaps I shouldn't have said that, eh. No, because I've got the best wife in England, there's no argument. But between you and me, my wife's the ugliest woman in the world. The ugliest woman in the world. I'd sooner take her with me than kiss her goodbye.

But then, marriage is a funny thing – Did I tell you about the deaf and dumb man who got married? He'd only been married a fortnight

and his wife made him wear boxing gloves in bed – to stop him talking in his sleep.

Now I've been married for years but mind you, I've only had two sweethearts in me life – two – it's enough, innit? No, honest, it's not a shame at all, 'cos it's nice, only two. No, I'm straight, dead straight, honest I am. As a butcher's hook!

Two sweethearts – the first was a telephone operator and the second, she was a schoolteacher. The first one, the telephone operator, she was hopeless. She kept saying 'Your three minutes are up.' But the schoolteacher, she was a smasher, wore glasses. I liked her wearing glasses. You know why ? I breathed on them, so she couldn't see what I was doing! Eventually – listen – eventually I married her and we had fifteen children. No, no, that's true. What, too many ? No, is it ? I don't know – Is it ? It is, isn't it ? And I told her, I told her. I said, 'Listen,' I said. 'Any more children,' I said, 'and I'll commit suicide.' She said, 'Don't be silly, Max, listen – come here.' I said, 'Any more' – spoke to her proper, you know – 'any more children, I'll commit suicide.' I came home – I'd been away to sea – I came home a few months after and she said, 'It's happened again.' I said, 'This is the end.' I went upstairs and I opened the drawers, and I got all me ties out, and tied them together, tied 'em round me neck, got on the table, other end tied to the gas lamp, and I was just going to jump off the table when I said to meself, 'Don't be a mug – you might be hanging the wrong man.'

Here's a funny thing – now this *is* a funny thing, I went home the other night – *that is* a funny thing, and I went in the back way, through the kitchen, through the dining-room to the drawing-room, and there's a fellow standing there, not a stitch on. He stood there with his hat in his hand – he looked like a bottle of Guinness. Well anyway, he hadn't got a stitch on, so I called the wife in. I said, 'Who's this ?' She said, 'Don't lose your temper, Miller, don't go raving mad.' I said, 'I'm only asking a fair question. Who is it ?' She said, 'He's a nudist and he's come in to use the phone.'

# —There's a clever one from the wife, eh?

But I must say in all honesty I've got the best wife in England. The other one's in Africa! She weighs twenty-eight stone. She goes dancing to get her weight down but I don't think it makes any difference. She's got the advantage of the slim girls when she's dancing – she doesn't have to shimmy like the slim girls 'cos she just walks quick, stops sudden, and lets nature takes its course.

But what does a woman care what her husband thinks? It's what the dressmaker thinks. If she can't wear the up-to-date model she might as well go without – and my wife goes without. I bought her a violin last week to give her chin a rest. My wife talks through her nose. A fellow said, 'What's the matter with her mouth?' I said, 'It's worn out.'

But my wife's a wonderful woman. Not good-looking – she's got one of those hard faces, if I may say so, a very hard face – all wrinkled. I think her mother was fond of walnuts. But apart from that she's all right. She's only got one eye – one eye, I must mention that – and every time I see her I sing to her 'You're the one I care for', which reminds me of the song that Nelson wrote: 'Please don't talk about me, one eye's gone'.

But she's a wonderful woman and I dedicate this song to her – accompanying myself on the guitar. (GUITAR CHORDS) Like a harp, innit ? It's got some volume, this has, listen – get some nice chords on this, can't you ? If you know where to put your fingers. No, well, it's tricky. It's not like a comb. Anybody can play a comb. No, this is clever stuff I'm giving you. Miller's the name, lady, there'll never be another, will there ? They don't make 'em today, duck. Boys will be boys, won't they ? Lucky for you girls,

# Otherwise
## you'd get
## no fun —

### No, Listen

Here's another one – It's called 'A Fan Dancer Minus Her Fan'. That's like, without, see, a fan dancer minus her fan. I haven't finished it yet, haven't finished it, I'm working on it now. I've got the beginning, and I've got a part of the end, but what I'm after is that middle bit, that's what I want. If I get that, I'll be all right. I'll give you a rough idea of what it's all about. I'm not going to give you a lot, you're not going to have a lot, 'cos I shall want it when I come back, you see.

> **I started courting a smashing fan dancer,**
> **To marry her that was my plan,**
> **Now it's all off with the smashing fan dancer –**
> **She fell down and damaged her fan.**

And I want it to go on like that. I want it to flow like that, all the time, keep moving all the time. It's the middle bit, that's what I'm after, the middle bit. I shall get it, it'll come to me, I shall get it – might come to me about four o'clock in the morning, you don't know. Well, that's when I get inspiration, that's when I write all my stuff, you see. If it does, I shall be out of bed quick, you know. Oh, write it all down, yes, write it down. Then the finish will be something like this, I'm not quite sure, but it'll be something like this:

> **Alas, that poor girl, she's gone home to her mother,**
> **Till her fan is mended or she gets another –**

– You know! And then you all come in with 'Oh dear, what can the matter be'. It'll be all right when I've finished it, won't it? Haven't got it finished yet.

Now when I started in this business many years ago, I started in a circus. I started in Billy Smart's circus – Billy Smart – not the Billy Smart who is today – his father – 'cos I'm much older than Billy. And I remember his father said to me one day, he said, 'Maxie, would you like to be a lion tamer?' I said, 'I've no desire.' He said, 'There's money in it.' I said, 'What do I have to do?' He said, 'All you've got to do is walk in the lion's cage and put your head in its mouth.' I said, 'I should think so.' He said, 'Are you scared?' I said, 'I'm not scared – I'm just careful.' He said, 'I shouldn't be scared of that lion,' he said, 'That lion's as tame as a kitten. He was brought up on milk.' I said,

# 'SO WAS I

# BUT I EAT MEAT !'

So he advertised for a lion tamer and a beautiful blonde came along, like they are today – you've seen 'em, well out in front – a lovely roll top desk – and that's a lot of madam an' all – that's the ironing board stuck up there. So he said to this blonde, 'Will you go into the cage?' She said, 'I'll go in, 'cos I'm a lion tamer.' And she walked into the cage, and as she walked into the cage the lion made a

dash for her and she thought quick, undid her zip and all her clothes
fell off her, and she stood there as naked as the day she was born, and
the lion, he stopped – then he started to walk towards her, and when
he got near enough he started to kiss her. And he kissed her all over,
and the governor said, 'Would you do that?' I said, 'Yes – get the
lion out!'

There was this little girl, she keeps biting her nails, and her mother says, 'Stop biting your nails because you know what'll happen to you?' She says, 'What'll happen to me?' Her mother says, 'You won't half get fat if you bite your nails.' She says, 'Well, I won't bite 'em any more, Mum.' Her mother took her shopping, got on the bus, and there's a fellow in a corner of the bus weighing about twenty stone. And she said, 'Mum, I'll get like that, won't I?' She said, 'You'll get worse than that, if you bite your nails.' She said, 'Well, I won't bite 'em any more.' And after shopping they got on another bus, and there's a blonde sitting in the corner, she's carrying a bit of weight as well –

– That's what I like about you, you're so quick.

You're

And the kiddie kept looking at the blonde and the blonde kept looking at the kiddie. And the blonde, she couldn't stand it any longer, so she said to the kiddie, 'Do you know me?' And the kiddie said, 'No, but I know what you've been doing!'

I love animals . . . I used to have a dog and I took him with me everywhere I went. One day a fellow came up to me and said, 'Max, that's a nice dog.' I said, 'He's very intelligent.' He said, 'What do you mean?' I said, 'If you give the dog a shilling he'll go and get the *Evening News* and bring back elevenpence change.' He said, 'Don't be foolish.' I said, 'Give the dog a shilling', and he gave the dog a shilling, and I said, 'Go on – *Evening News*.' And away went the dog. We waited for half an hour – the dog didn't come back. He said, 'Where's your dog?' I said, 'I don't know, he's never done it before. Never done it before,' I said, 'We'd better go and look for him.' And we went along Piccadilly, and there was my dog walking along Piccadilly with his girlfriend. I said, 'I don't understand it, he's never done it before.' My pal said, 'Well, perhaps he's never had the money.'

Of course, that was years ago. And talking of years ago . . .

. . . there was this old couple, an old couple sitting round the fire – and she said, 'What's the matter, Jim?' and he said, 'Jean, I was thinking, it's our Golden Wedding today, and wouldn't it be lovely if we could go to Bournemouth and stay at the same hotel as we did fifty years ago today?' She said, 'Why shouldn't we?' – she was game – so they got on their tandem and away they went and they got to Bournemouth. She said, 'Here we are in the same room, the same surroundings, the same pictures on the wall, everything the same as it was fifty years ago today.' She said, 'Don't you remember how eager you were to kiss me? You didn't give me time to get me stockings off,' and he said,

'You'll have plenty of time tonight to knit yourself a pair!'

# Passing the Time Away

I know exactly – I know exactly what you're saying to yourselves.
You're wrong – I know what you're saying – oh you, you wicked lot!
You're the kind of people who'll get me a bad name!

*Oh that girl was very nice,*
*She didn't take her ma's advice,*
*Once she did the same thing twice,*
*Passing the time away.*

*Her boyfriend took her to Southend,*
*For the afternoon to spend,*
*She must have stayed the whole weekend,*
*Passing the time away.*

*He took her on the sands,*
*Then he took her on the pier –*
*He was in the navy*
*So he had the right idea.*

*Though she lives next door to me,*
*She's as sweet as sweet can be,*
*Now she's worried, I can see,*
*Through passing the time away.*

Now I'd like to do 'Mary Ann'. Before I sing the song I feel I should tell you something about it, otherwise you won't know what it's all about, because in Russia, many years ago, they did – and I think they do now – I think so – they did everything on the five-year plan. Made no difference what it was – yes, they got married on the five-year plan, they made love on the five-year plan – everything was on the five-year plan. And I told my girlfriend about it. And I'll tell you about it in my song – 'The Five-Year Plan'.

# The Five-Year Plan

*Mary Ann, Mary Ann,*
*Let us get together on the five-year plan.*
*We'll both go off to business*
*Every morning, 'twill be fine,*
*I'll bring my wages home*
*And maybe you'll put yours to mine.*
(VARIATION : *And you can put your bit to mine.*)


– Go on, make something of that – go on, make something of it!
Filthy lot – filthy!


*You say you cannot sleep at night,*
*Your bed is no temptation,*
*Say the word and marry me*
*And I'll be your salvation.*
*I'll take your Horlicks up to bed*
*And stop your night starvation –*

*Mary Ann, Mary Ann,*
*We'll both be as loving as we can.*
*You'll feel a little strange at first,*
*But then you needn't bother,*
*As long as you can get a few*
*Good wrinkles from your mother,*
*And go back home again*
*When we get tired of one another –*
*Wouldn't it be lovely, Mary Ann ?*

*Mary Ann, Mary Ann,*
*Let us get together on the five-year plan.*
*If you leave me then you'll be free,*
*There's no need to divorce me.*
*I'll let you have the children, too,*
*You wouldn't have to force me.*

*Mary Ann, Mary Ann, .*
*We'll both be as happy as we can.*
*The coffee beans each morning*
*For your breakfast I will grind up,*
*Before I go to bed I'll bolt the door,*
*The clock I'll wind up,*
*And that will give you tons of time*
*For you to make your mind up –*
*Wouldn't it be lovely, Mary Ann ?*

# I don't care what I say, do I?

I don't, I don't care, honest I don't!

I look better since I came back off my *cruise*, don't I? No, well, I did look poorly, wasn't I poorly? No, I was, I was dying, before I went away. I look nice now, don't I, duck, don't I? No, I feel better, too. I liked it. It was nice. I'm going again next year. I want to go every year if I can, 'cos it's nice. I had a cabin to meself. All the time I was there, a cabin to meself. And next to me there was an old maid. She had a cabin to herself, too. So I was all right, wasn't I? Well, no, no . . . What, *me*? I don't, I don't. No, honest I don't, I don't. Well, when I say that –

Look – and one night this old maid she started screaming and banging on her door, kicking up a terrible noise. And the purser came along and said, 'What's going on in there?' She said, 'There are two men in my room.' He said, 'Well, what do you want me to do?' She said, 'Sling one of them out.' So he slung me – here, listen!

Come here, listen, listen. What is an old maid ? That is the question.
A bundle of sour discontent.


**If you were to offer her sweet married bliss,**
**She'd want this and that and then want that and this;**
**Then if you gave her just what she wanted,**
**Don't think a favour you do her,**
**Because after she got what she wanted, she wouldn't want**
**it, so what's the good of giving it –**


listen – listen.

Are you listening ?

– I mean, it's a waste –

no, it's a waste of time,

innit, lady ?

Listen –


**They took the vanity from the peacock,**
**The cunning from the fox,**
**The brains from a jackass,**
**The jawbone from an ox,**
**The venom from the viper,**
**The stinger from the bee –**
**Put them all in my old woman**
**And bunged her on to me.**

Of course, I shouldn't say that really. It isn't fair – because I've just come back from my holidays – and I always have a wonderful time when I go on my holidays because I haven't got one of those wives who says 'Where have you been? How much have you spent? Who have you been with?' She doesn't say that – she comes with me. But she didn't go with me this time – I went to Africa, the north of Africa. Where the camels are. I stayed on the desert five weeks – five weeks on the desert! – I'm a real sheikh – I'll go in anybody's tent tonight. You put up a tent, lady, and try me! I'll go in, I'm no trouble – I carry me own sand – here!

Listen – do you know the first thing I saw in the desert? A mummy. I think she was looking for her daddy. She came straight up to me and said, 'Pharoah, my Pharoah.' I said, 'I'm not your Pharoah.' She said,

'Who are you ?' I said, 'I'm Mrs Miller's youngest son and I've come out here for peace and quietness.'

She looked at me – she kept looking into my eyes. What was she after – me lashes ? No, no, 'cos I've got big eyes, look – that's me mother's fault – looking all over England for me father. Listen, listen. She looked into my eyes and she said, 'For two thousand years I have waited for this moment. I am a flame of fire.' 'For two thousand years ?' I said, 'You must be hungry. I'll get you some dates.'

Listen. She looked into my eyes and she said, 'Whither thou goest I goeth also whither thou.' I said, 'How far have we got to go, lady ?' She said, 'Half a league', and when we got there I was in the second division. Playing for Chelsea.

We started to walk across the desert – no, turn it up, what's the matter with you – no, well . . . No, when a chap's talking – no, it's true . . . well . . . Git out of it! Well . . . We started to walk across the desert – five days and five nights we were walking. We came to a tent – we stood outside the tent – I wouldn't go in – two thousand years old, she was!

# — here!

We stood outside the tent and she said, 'Thy people shall be my people and my people shall be thy people', and she opened the tent – blimey! They could have been anybody's. I never saw so many people in one tent in my life. There were nine hundred of them in the tent. Nine hundred in one tent. All sitting on ottomans. And what a crowd they are, the Ottomans. Dead cunning, they are, the Ottomans. They're worse than the Pyramids. And *they're* tricky, you know. So I thought to meself as I walked in the tent, I thought they were going to say, 'Hello, Max.' Like they do round here when they're on the tap – I don't care, I don't care a poppy. And they all stood up, nine hundred of them, with little short shirts on no longer than that – some of the men were taller – here!

They all stood up and they said, "All hail, all hail!' – that was the limit, see – what kind of people are you, tonight? I thought to meself, 'There's going to be a party here.' So I stayed, and I had some of this ale – well – no, I didn't have a lot – I didn't take a lot, y'see – and in the morning I was so drunk I found meself up a gum tree shaking hands with some of the palms, see. So the two thousand year old, she came along and she said, 'Leave that alone.'

'Course, I twigged what she meant. No, no, no – what, me? I don't, I don't. No, honest, I don't, I don't. No, I was on another branch then, see. And I thought she was going to say, 'All hail, all hail', but she didn't. She said, 'Achoo, achoo, all fall down.' Well, we fell down, see, and I wanted to teach her a game that I knew, see, so I looked at her and I said, 'Have you had a wash this morning?' She said, 'No.' I said, 'Why?' She said, 'We can't get any water.' I said, 'Well, how do you keep yourselves clean?' She said, 'We smother ourselves with oil.' And she was speaking the truth, because every time I went to kiss her I felt myself slipping, see – I'm bad enough, you don't have to bother, lady! So I looked at her and I said, 'I'd like to woo you.' – Yes, I told her, I was there! I was there, y'see. She said, 'What?' I said, 'I'd like to woo you.' She said, 'You can't woo me.' I said. 'Why not?' She said, 'I don't woo.' 'Listen,' I said, 'I'll tell you what I'll do,' I said. 'Being a man of the world, I'll marry you. I've got me bike – I can get away, see.' She said, 'You can't marry me unless you ask my father.' I said, 'How old's your father?' She said, 'He's three thousand years old and he's got a hundred and fifty wives.' I said, 'A hundred and fifty?' She said, 'Yes.' I said, 'Where is he?' She said, 'This is him coming along on a stretcher.'

*– No, no, no – he'd got gout.*

Well, when he got up to me he said, 'What do you think of my daughter?' I said, 'I think she's very nice. I'd like to marry her.' He said, 'You can't marry my daughter unless you give me three cows.' Now, there's a man with a hundred and fifty wives – you can't get 'em out there, there's nowhere to graze, y'see. No – it's all sand, it's all sand for miles. We use it for bird cages, I sweep it up now and then.

But I tell you something they taught me in the desert. They taught me about woman –

Woman – an angel of truth, a demon of fiction,
Woman's the greatest of all contradictions;
Afraid of a wasp, she'll scream at a mouse,
She'll attack the husband who's big as a house,
She'll take him for better, she'll take him for worse,
She'll break open his head and then be his nurse.
And when he is well and can get out of bed,
She'll take up the saucepan and shy at his head.
Hateful, deceitful, keen-sighted, blind,
Crafty, simple, cruel and kind,
Lifts a man up, casts a man down,
Makes him a king then makes him a clown;
In the morning she will, in the evening she won't,
And you're always expecting she does,

# but she don't

A woman comes into a man's life like a ray of sunshine – and goes through his pockets like a flash of lightning. I know, 'cos I know what I'm talking about.

And don't talk to me about women . . .

I was going home the other morning at daybreak – *daybreak* – I wouldn't venture out at night. I was going along a country road and I saw a young lady. She was coming towards me. When she got right up near me I looked at her and I said, 'Can I see you home?' She said, 'No, I'm going the other way.' I said, 'I can turn round.' So I turned round, see, I turned round, and we started to walk in the middle of the road. I said, 'Let's get up on the path.' So we got up on the path, and there was all grass on the path, all grass, so I bent down and felt the grass and I said, 'Some dew!'

And she said,

# 'Some don't.

# Good
# MORNING!'

– Now listen!

Then I met a young lady pushing a pram. I've known this young lady twenty-five years, and I said to her, 'I see you have a baby now.' She said, 'Yes.' I said, 'I thought you were an old maid?' She said, 'So I am but I'm not narrow-minded.'

Then she said, 'Do you mind if I sit down, 'cos I'm pregnant?' I said, 'You don't look it. How long have you been pregnant?' She said, 'Only ten minutes but doesn't it make you tired?'

Her name was Lulu. What a lovely name – and what a lovely girl.

*Lulu, I know that you do*
*Think that I've been fooling all along.*
*No matter what I do,*
*I somehow know that you*
*Always seem to get me wrong.*

*Lulu, I wouldn't fool you,*
*I'm always saying nice things to you.*
*I'll take you in the country*
*Each Sunday for a trip,*
*And as we climb the hills*
*I'll walk behind in case you slip.*

*Lulu, I wouldn't fool you,*
*In anything I say or do.*
*I'll take you to the seaside*
*Not very far from town,*
*And as we lay upon the sands*
*We'll both get nice and brown,*
*And if the sun should scorch your back*
*I'll always turn you round –*
*I wouldn't fool you, Lulu.*

*Lulu, I wouldn't fool you,*
*When in a swimming pool, to cool you*
*I'll dive right off the deep end*
*Because I've got the knack,*
*Then I can do the breast stroke*
*While you're floating on your back.*

*Lulu, I wouldn't fool you,*
*In anything I say or do,*
*We'll swim around together,*
*You'll like it I am sure,*
*We'll stay beneath the water*
*For half an hour or more,*
*Then I can teach you lots of strokes*
*You've never done before –*
*I wouldn't fool you, Lulu.*

Ah – Lulu. I met her in Paris. She was a blonde, and a friend came up to me and he said, 'Be careful of the blondes,' he said, 'They're more loving than brunettes.' 'Well,' I said, 'I don't know about that,' I said, 'My wife's been both and I haven't noticed the difference.' But then Lulu said to me, she said, 'I'm a married woman with fourteen children.' I said, 'Well?' She said, 'My husband, he doesn't love me. Don't you think I'm unfortunate?' I said, 'Unfortunate?' I said, 'Think what would have happened if he *had* loved you!'

Of course, I know all about love. Mind you, I didn't always know. I remember when I was twenty-one, my mother said to my father, she said, 'Jim,' she said. 'What, Jean?' he said. She said, 'The lad's twenty-one today. He's going out into the world among the birds and flowers, and I think it's only right we should tell him everything he ought to know.' And my mother came up into my room, and she knelt down at my bed – I was having my breakfast at the time, 'cos I don't get up very early. I'll give you a rough idea what time I get up – my morning paper's the *Evening News*, that's the time I get up. She said, 'Son, you're going out into the world and I'm going to tell you everything.' I said, 'Go on, Mother, tell me. I have no shame, tell me.' She said, 'It's not Father Christmas who puts the toys in your stocking.'

Of course, I knew all the time – I'll tell you why, because one morning when I woke up I found a bicycle in my stocking and I was riding down the road and I knocked a poor old lady over, and when she picked herself up she said to me, 'Can't you ring the bell?' I said, 'Yes, I can ring the bell, but I can't ride the bike.'

I was so upset I could have cried for her, I could really, I could have cried. And they took me to the hospital, and when I got to the hospital, the doctor said, 'You've broken your arm.' I said, 'Well, doctor, tell me, after my arm's better will I be able to play the piano?' He said, 'Yes.' I said, 'That's funny, I couldn't play it before.'

Children are funny though, aren't they? There was this father and son. Boy'd be about eight or nine – he might be nine or ten, we don't know, who cares anyway? Eight or nine. His father took him round a cattle show on a Saturday afternoon when the farmers were buying the bulls and the cows – mostly bulls – when all of a sudden the little boy saw a farmer go up to a bull, and the farmer started feeling the bull, all along the back he was feeling it, all down and all round, feeling all over. And the little boy said, 'Daddy, what's he doing?' And his father told him. He said, 'He's feeling it to see if there's any meat on it. If there's any meat on it, he's going to buy it.' So the boy said, 'Thanks very much, Father, for telling me.' Two or three weeks after, the boy went to see his father. His father was having breakfast. His father said, 'What do you want?' The boy said, 'I think the butler wants to buy the cook.'

There was a feller, a feller who won £75,000 on the pools, and his father said, 'Son, what are you going to do with all that money?' He said, 'Dad, I'm going to give you a pound to start with.' His father said, 'A pound!' He said, 'A pound – you lousy – a pound?' He said, 'What are you going to do with the rest?' The son said, 'I'm going to get married and go all round the world then come back and settle down.' He said, 'Dad, what are you going to do with your pound?' He looked straight at the boy, looked him right in the eyes, and said,

'Son, I'm going to marry your mother.'

No, but I must tell you. A pal of mine – a master builder – said to his little boy round about Christmas time, 'What would you like for Christmas?' So the boy said, 'I'd like a baby brother.' So the master builder said, 'We couldn't finish the job in time.' He said, 'You can have a gun or a horse', and the boy said, 'No, I don't want a gun, and I don't want a horse. I want a baby brother.' The fellow said, 'I told you, we can't finish the job in time', and the boy said, 'Well, you can put some more men on the job.'

You may not believe this, but I've been a bit of a bad lad in my time, and I remember many years ago I said to my brother, 'Johnny, I've got a confession to make. I've been with a woman.' He said, 'Well, go in and tell father', so I went into the drawing-room to see me dad, he was in a deckchair. I said, 'Dad, I've got a confession to make.' He said, 'What is it, son?' And I said, 'Dad, I've made love to a married woman.' He said, 'Tell me, who was it?' I wouldn't tell him. He said, 'Was it Mrs Graham at No. 19?' I said, 'No, no.' He said, 'Was it Mrs Mitchell at No. 23?' I said, 'No' – I wouldn't crack on, y'see. He said, 'Was it Mrs Smith at No. 47?' I said, 'No.' He said, 'Get out of the room! I'm disgusted with you.' So I walked out of the room and my brother said, 'How did you get on? Did he forgive you?' I said, 'No, but he gave me three very good addresses!'

I said to my father, I said, 'Dad, I want to get married.' He said, 'All right son, who do you want to marry?' I said, 'I'd like to marry Miss Green.' He said, 'You can't.' I said, 'Why not?' He said, 'She's your half-sister. When I was a lad I had a bike and I got around a bit.' I said, 'All right, I'll marry Miss White.' He said, 'You can't. She's your half-sister. Forget about it.' Well, I was a bit despondent and I walked around. My mum said to me, 'What's wrong with you?' I said, 'Well, I said to Dad I wanted to marry Miss Green and he said I couldn't because she's my half-sister. I said, "All right, I'll marry Miss White." He said, "You can't. She's your half-sister." ' She said, 'Look, you go and marry which one you like. He's not your father anyway!'

But I'm a big lad now. Yes. I'm an artist now, lady – I've got my own studios at Brighton, and a woman came to my house – half past ten on Monday morning. She said, 'Max, I want you to paint a snake on my knee.' I went dead white, honest I did. No, well, I'm not strong, I'm not strong. So, listen, I jumped into bed – no, listen a minute – so I started to paint a snake. Just above her knee, that's where I started. But I had to chuck it – she smacked me in the face. I didn't know a snake was so long – how long's an ordinary snake ?


We're coming to the last of the Blue Book. It says here – 'Hints on etiquette. How to drink a cocktail and what to do with the cherry.'

# That's nice, innit?

Now here's one – This man gets a telegram and he says, 'I'm happy today. I'm a daddy. I'm a daddy – after eighteen years I'm a daddy. And before the happy event my wife went to see a fortune-teller. The fortune teller told her, "If it's a boy the father will die. If it's a girl the mother will die." I've got a letter here from me mother-in-law on me father's side. I'll read it to you – from me mother-in-law. It says:

"Your wife has presented you with a bouncing baby boy. Both doing well."

That'll tell you what the fortune-teller knows. Here am I, strong as a lion, game for anything. She goes on to say:

"PS – Sorry to say the milkman dropped dead this morning." '

Thank you very much, ladies and gentlemen, thank you very much. Now, people have asked me to finish with a straight song, so I've written one and it's called 'Be Sincere', a beautiful song, beautifully sung. Miller's the name, lady.

There'll never be another –

# Be Sincere

When roses are red,
They're ready for plucking.
When a girl is sixteen,
She's ready for . . . .

# 'ERE!